This book is on loan from
Library Services for Schools
**www.cumbria.gov.uk/
libraries/schoolslibserv**

County Council

Looking at...
ANIMAL CRUELTY

Chris Mason

WAYLAND

First published in 2009 by Wayland

Copyright © Wayland 2009

Wayland
338 Euston Road
London NW1 3BH

Wayland Australia
Level 17/207 Kent Street
Sydney NSW 2000

Produced for Wayland by
White-Thomson Publishing Ltd

+44 (0) 845 362 8240
www.wtpub.co.uk

Editors: Sonya Newland and Katie Powell
Designer: Robert Walster

Mason, Chris
    Looking at animal cruelty
    1. Animal welfare - Juvenile literature
    I. Title II. Animal cruelty
    179.3

ISBN: 9780750259019

Picture Credits
AKG Berlin: 8; Associated Press: 35 (Michel Euler),
39 (Denis Poroy), 43 (Louise Buller); Camera Press:
4 (Brian Snyder), 16 (J. Kopec); Corbis: 33 (Dan
Chung/Reuters); James Davis Travel Photography: 18;
Dreamstime: 14 (Barsik); Durrell Wildlife Conservation
Trust: 37; Ecoscene: *contents* bottom (Michael Gore),
7, 26 (Sally Morgan), 34 (Michael Gore); Family Life
Pictures: 19 top (Angela Hampton); FLPA: 30 (Terry
Whittaker); Getty Images: 12 (Altrendo Images), 20
(David Aubrey); Robert Harding Picture Library: 20
bottom (R. Maisonneuve), 25 (Kodak), 36 bottom, 44
(Bildagentur Schuster); Hodder Wayland Picture
Library: 6 bottom, 19 bottom, 23 bottom; Impact: 22
(Bruce Stephens), 42 (Philippe Gontier); iStock: *cover*
(Sondra Paulson), 21 (Iain Sarjeant), 40 (Jennifer
Daley); Panos Pictures: *contents* top, 17; Popperfoto:
10 (John Hrusa, Reuters), 11 (Corinne Dufka, Reuters),
13 (Andrew Winning), 15 (Jason Reed, Reuters), 24, 32
(Paul Hackett, Reuters); RSPCA Photolibrary: 5, 6 top,
9 (Philip Meech), 28 (Nathan Strange), 31, 33 top, 38
(Louise Murray/Wild Images); Science Photo Library:
45 (Simon Fraser); Still Pictures: 27 (Dylan Garcia),
29 (Matthew Wanner), 41 (Peter Weimann); Topham
Picturepoint: 23 top.

Printed in China

Wayland is a division of Hachette Children's Books,
an Hachette UK company.
www.hachette.co.uk

CONTENTS

How can people do that?

Have you ever been cruel? Perhaps – but it was a little thing and you didn't mean it. Would you be cruel to animals? The answer is probably 'no'. Most of you will answer these questions in a similar way.

Cruelty and prevention

We all say or do cruel things sometimes, but we soon learn that it causes pain and suffering. Most people regret doing that, especially to animals. However, not

'I think that the worst kind of cruelty is being unfair to animals when you're fed up with them and can't be bothered. If you have a pet, you have to realize how you've got to change when you get one.'

GEORGE COOPER, 12, WHO HAS A WIRE-HAIRED FOX TERRIER CALLED BOB

← A hunter clubbing a seal to death in Canada. The animals are killed so people can use their fur and other body parts.

everyone thinks this way, and some people are deliberately cruel to animals. Governments and charities around the world work hard to protect animals from being harmed by people. Despite this, thousands of cases of cruelty to animals are reported worldwide.

⬆ This pony was left to starve to death by his owners. Luckily, he was rescued by the RSPCA, an animal charity.

What is cruelty?

Every year in Canada, more than 250,000 seals are killed for their meat and fur. Many people have campaigned to stop this, but not everybody agrees that it is cruel, so seal-hunting continues. Some people believe that the hunters do not cause unnecessary pain.

Why are people cruel?

Some people treat their pets badly or just neglect them. Other people may be cruel to farm animals. Some people might hurt animals just for fun.

Some people do not mean to be cruel, they just do not understand what they are doing. In some cases, people cause pain and suffering to their pets because they do not know how to look after them. Ignorance like this is one of the main causes of cruelty to pets all over the world.

⬆ Large animals, like this bear in Borneo, seem unhappy living in cramped conditions such as cages.

⬅ A catch of fish from a trawler being sorted by fishermen. Pictures like this are common, but many people argue that fishing is cruel to animals.

Different points of view

Other people simply do not believe that what they are doing is cruel. Some people who hunt or fish cause pain and suffering to wild animals. But they do not see hunting or fishing as cruel – they think it is necessary. They are often very upset if people call them cruel.

So why are people cruel to animals? What is cruel and what isn't? Can we stop people being cruel? This book will help you answer the questions for yourself.

⬇ Pilot whales are killed for their meat in the Faeroe Islands. The islanders think this is an acceptable practice.

CASE STUDY ▸ CASE STUDY ▸ CASE STUDY ▸ CASE STUDY ▸

Every year, the people of the Faeroe Islands in the North Atlantic carry out the *Grindadrap*, the hunting and killing of up to 1,500 pilot whales. This is a tradition that goes back hundreds of years. The whales are driven to the shore by powerboats and then killed with special long knives. Many people think the hunt is cruel, but the islanders disagree. They ask, 'What is more humane: to have an animal living in a cage all its life, or to let it roam free from birth to death? Do you think that going to the clean, disinfected supermarket for your meat is more natural than a bloody and messy hunt?'

Caring for animals

People have always lived close to animals. Early humans hunted animals for food. Later, they started keeping and breeding animals to kill for food. We do not know when people first started keeping animals as pets, but pictures from early times show what seem to be tame dogs and cats.

⬇ An American coal miner photographed with a pit pony in the nineteenth century. The animals had to endure harsh working conditions.

Cats in ancient Egypt

The ancient Egyptians kept and even worshipped cats. They would mourn the death of a cat and punish people who harmed them. There is even a legend that tells how the Egyptians surrendered a city to their enemy, the Persians, to save hundreds of cats that the Persian army had captured.

Animal-welfare organizations

Organizations such as the American Society for the Prevention of Cruelty to Animals (ASPCA) and the Royal

Society for the Prevention of Cruelty to Animals (RSPCA) in Britain were established during the nineteenth century. The people who set up these charities were horrified by the way domestic and farm animals were being treated.

They put together teams of inspectors who could take people to court if they were cruel to animals. They also set up places to care for animals that were ill or had been abandoned. Today, these animal-welfare organizations still help educate people about animal cruelty, and work to prevent it.

⬇ An RSPCA inspector examining a pet rabbit. Animal-welfare charities like the RSPCA can show people how to treat animals properly.

FACT

The Society for the Prevention of Cruelty to Animals (SPCA) was founded in the UK in 1824. In that year it had 149 people convicted for cruelty. The Royal Society for the Prevention of Cruelty to Animals (RSPCA), as it is now known, investigated more than 122,000 cases of suspected cruelty in England and Wales in 2007.

RSPCA ONLINE.

The PDSA

In 1917, Maria Dickin set up the People's Dispensary for Sick Animals (PDSA) in London. Maria was shocked by the suffering of animals that belonged to poor people, who could not afford to pay for a vet. She opened a free clinic to help these sick animals.

⬇ Helpers release some African penguins that were cleaned up after an oil spill off Cape Town, South Africa.

The PDSA now has 43 PetAid hospitals throughout the UK. These treat more than a million pets a year, belonging to people who cannot afford to pay for a vet if their pet gets ill.

CASE STUDY ▸ CASE STUDY ▸ CASE STUDY ▸ CASE STUDY ▸

In June 2000, an oil spill off Cape Town, South Africa, threatened thousands of African penguins on Robben and Dassen islands. Among the volunteers who helped with rescuing and washing the affected birds were many students from local schools. Younger children like Rachel and Shannon Bernhardt, and their friend Kaya Kuhn, produced a newsletter called 'Penguin Post', and organized collections of money to help the rescue effort.

Educating children

PDSA also runs Pet Protectors, a club that teaches children from the age of five about responsible pet ownership. Teenagers also support the organization's work through the PDSA Youth Challenge.

The IFAW

The International Fund for Animal Welfare (IFAW) is an international campaigning organization. It uses protests and publicity to stop cruelty, particularly the killing of wild animals such as whales and elephants. It also works to protect the habitat of wild animals, and rescues animals in distress after disasters such as oil spills.

'It's time to say "enough", and insist that our coastlines, their communities and the animals that live there are properly protected.'
SARAH SCARTH, IFAW's EMERGENCY RELIEF CO-ORDINATOR, AFTER A LARGE OIL SPILL OFF THE SOUTH AFRICAN COAST

⬇ A huge pile of confiscated ivory being burned by the Kenya Wildlife Service.

Animals that help people

Sometimes animals look after us – for example, seeing-eye dogs for the blind and dogs used in search-and-rescue missions. There are many true stories of how dolphins have guided people to shore to save them from drowning.

⬇ There is a special relationship between seeing-eye dogs and their owners because the owner must trust the dog completely.

A special bond

In all different cultures, there are tales of how animals have helped people. There are stories of how fish helped villagers in West Africa to find water during a drought, and how an old wolf kept a dying man company in Russia. Native Americans have many stories about special bonds between people and animals.

Animals for therapy

Today, animals are often used to help people with illnesses or disabilities. In the USA, there are over 2,500 programmes using animals in this way.

Helping disabled children

A horse called Pete is one of the animals used for therapy. He suffered neglect and cruelty, but he was rescued and taken to the Cape Cod Therapeutic Riding Center in the USA. Now Pete works at the centre, helping children with disabilities.

Pete is particularly sensitive to the needs of children who have either Down's syndrome or cerebral palsy, making up for their poor balance or lack of control. No one at the centre doubts the benefits to the children of riding on Pete.

⬆ A child with learning difficulties has therapy with a dolphin at a Mexican zoo.

Are pets companions or victims?

Billions of pounds in total are spent on pets every year in wealthy countries such as the UK and the USA. This shows how important pets, or companion animals, are to people in these countries.

Pampered pets

Pets are not just fed scraps any more. Pet owners can now buy special 'gourmet' and 'diet' food for their pets. Some people even

⬇ People around the world love their pets, but you must think about the needs of the animal before buying it.

buy jewellery for pets such as cats and dogs, or dress them up in small coats. There are also special salons where people can take their pets to be groomed.

Killing with kindness

Sometimes, though, people who love their pets can do them harm without realizing it. More and more dogs and cats have to be treated for weight problems, because their owners are feeding them too much and not giving them enough exercise.

⬆ This poodle is taking part in a dog-grooming show in Thailand.

Humans and animals

Some of the animals that we keep as pets are not suited to living with people. For example, rabbits prefer fresh air to a hutch indoors. Just tapping on a fish tank with your fingers can scare a goldfish. Hamsters like to live in holes, and may be so afraid when picked up that they have a heart attack.

FACT

In a recent survey of dog and cat owners in the USA, 93 per cent of them said that they felt their pet was a real member of the family, and 95 per cent said that their own happiness was directly affected by the happiness of their pet.

PetSmart, 2008.

Exotic pets

Some people like to keep exotic pets. These are unusual animals such as spiders, snakes, turtles and even monkeys. Exotic pets can be very difficult to look after because they often come from very different habitats from ours. They may need to be kept very warm and to be fed on special food – sometimes other animals.

Many exotic-pet owners look after their animals well, but some find that they cannot cope. If this happens, they may release their pets into the wild, where they soon become ill and die.

⬇ This owner keeps an unusual mixture of pets, including a dog, a warthog and a lioness.

Endangered animals

Trade in exotic pets is growing. Rare animals, sometimes ones that are in danger of extinction, may be popular with collectors. People earn a lot of money by capturing and selling rare monkeys, reptiles, wild cats and birds to collectors.

Illegal trade

Trade in these animals is against the law, and people work hard to stop rare animals being caught and sold. Despite this, the trade continues. Many animals suffocate or starve while being transported to other countries.

⬆ A variety of small mammals are crammed into cages at an animal market in China.

CASE STUDY ▸ CASE STUDY ▸ CASE STUDY ▸ CASE STUDY ▸

Customs officers in the Philippines discovered two drills — rare rainforest monkeys from Africa — in a smuggled consignment of exotic pets bound for collectors in Asia. Animal-welfare organizations, with the help of the Philippines government, the airline Lufthansa and the oil company Mobil, arranged for them to be sent to a refuge in Nigeria. Within a year, the drills were ready to be released back into the wild. Everyone involved was surprised and pleased when one of the drills gave birth just before she was released back into her natural habitat.

On the farm

In 2008, there were more than 6.7 billion people on Earth. Most of them, especially those who live in towns and cities – more than half the world's population – rely on farmers to provide them with food.

Eating meat

People who live in wealthy countries such as the UK, Canada and the USA are eating more meat than ever before. Other countries, such as India, are starting to follow this trend, as more and more fast-food restaurants are being set up. Because of this, farmers are having to produce more meat, and it has to be cheap otherwise people will not buy it.

FACT

Every year over 100 million pigs are raised in the USA. Sometimes up to 10,000 pigs are kept in one huge building.

FACTORYFARMING.COM AND THE NEWS & OBSERVER, RALEIGH, NORTH CAROLINA.

⬇ Food stands like this cater to people who want their food fast and cheap.

Traditional and modern farms

The farms that produce animal products like pork, beef, chickens, eggs and milk are not like the traditional picture we might have of farms. Often they are not just a few small buildings and barns, and some fields with small herds of cows, or chickens roaming the farmyard.

To meet the growing demand for cheap meat and to make a profit, there are now 'factory farms'. These may have hundreds or even thousands of animals kept in small cages or pens in a factory unit. The more animals there are in a unit, the more efficient the farm will be, and the more money it will make.

⬆ Many modern farms exist to produce meat for sale in butcher's shops.

⬇ Not all farms look like this; many are run more like factories.

Arguments against factory farming

Many people believe that factory or intensive farming – where animals are raised in ways that get the most meat, milk or eggs from them – is cruel. Cows, which have a natural lifespan of 20 to 25 years, may produce more milk when they are raised on intensive farms, but they may only live around five years before 'burning out'.

Hens kept in battery cage systems may live four hens to one tiny cage. They cannot flap their wings or exercise their legs. The shed in which they live may have no windows, and could hold up to 90,000 birds. The European Union (EU) is now replacing battery production with systems that allow hens more space and some freedom.

↑ Battery hens may be kept in cages that have a floor the size of a piece of A4 paper.

← In intensive farming, many routine operations, such as feeding cows, are done by machines.

← Free-range chickens enjoy much better living conditions than poultry kept in battery cages.

What is free-range farming?

Because many people think that battery or intensive farming is cruel, more farmers are using a method called free range. In this system the animals have more room if they are kept indoors, and are allowed to roam around more when they are outside.

Free-range chickens

Although free-range chickens may be kept on perches in barns, often in large numbers, they are able to move freely both within the barn and outdoors. They can behave as birds naturally do and have room to stretch and flap their wings.

'We give our animals good, home-grown food, plenty of fresh air, roomy and well-bedded winter quarters and as short a journey to market as possible, because we want them to live as well as they can without stress or suffering.'

RUTH AND MIKE DOWNHAM, ORGANIC FARMERS IN CUMBRIA, UK

Farming the seas

Many people think that fish farming, or aquaculture, is a good way of providing food for the growing global population without being cruel to animals. People have farmed fish for centuries in Asia and parts of Africa.

What is fish farming?

Instead of being caught in the wild, fish and shellfish are raised in floating pens fixed to the bottom of the river or sea. The fish are bred in hatcheries and then raised in larger pens, where they are fed special food. When they are fully grown, the fish are taken from the pens, killed and then sold as food. About a quarter of the world's supply of fish is now produced on fish farms.

FACT

Fish farming is one of the fastest-growing agricultural industries in the world. One in five fish eaten by people is produced in a fish farm.

FOOD AND AGRICULTURE ORGANIZATION OF THE UNITED NATIONS.

← A salmon hatchery in Scotland. Once the fish have hatched, they are reared in pens until they are ready to be sold for food.

Is fish farming cruel?

Some people feel that fish farming is cruel.
Salmon are carnivores, which means that they
eat other sea creatures in the wild. On fish
farms, they have to be fed special food made
from other fish and shellfish. It can take up to
5 kg of wild fish to raise 1 kg of farmed fish.

Pollution and other problems

The uneaten food, fish waste and the chemicals
used to treat the fish can cause a lot of
pollution. The fish are crowded into pens and
have none of the freedom they enjoy in the
wild. At feeding time, when the overcrowding
is worst, the fish can be injured or even killed.

↑ Wild salmon are
naturally strong; those
bred in fish farms live
in cramped conditions.

← Up to 20 per cent
of the fish you might
see at the fishmongers
may have been raised
on fish farms.

Animals on show

Many children first see large animals, such as tigers, bears and elephants, in circuses. It can be exciting to see these animals in real life, rather than in pictures or on the television, but many people feel that making animals perform in circuses is cruel.

⬇ This chimpanzee, dressed up as a football player, has been taught to perform tricks.

All the fun of the circus?

In the wild, elephants do not stand upright on tubs. Wild bears do not ride little bikes. Tigers do not jump through flaming hoops.

Circus animals have to be trained to do the tricks that people expect to see. This training can be cruel and unnatural. When they are not performing, the animals may be kept in cramped cages or wagons that are quite different from their natural environment.

Unnatural behaviour

Some people believe that circuses make us see wild animals in the wrong way. An elephant in a dress loses its natural dignity. In the wild, a female elephant may lead a family for decades. It is free to roam the land, and forms deep and caring relationships. Spending a life in chains and performing tricks is not natural behaviour.

People who support circuses say that they allow visitors to see animals that they would not otherwise see close up. Others argue that it would be better not to see them at all.

'I think these elephants are trying to tell us that zoos and circuses are not what God created them for. But we have not been listening.'

POLICE OFFICER BLAYNE DOYLE, WHO HAD TO SHOOT AN ESCAPED CIRCUS ELEPHANT

← Lots of people enjoy seeing wild animals in a circus, but others think that making animals perform like this takes away their dignity.

At the zoo

The earliest zoo that we know about was set up by the ancient Egyptian Queen Hatshepsut. She filled her zoo with exotic animals, and used it to show off her wealth and power.

The menagerie at the Tower of London was created by King John in the twelfth century. It was opened to the public in the seventeenth century, and people visited it to watch the animal baiting.

In France at about the same time, King Louis XIV opened his zoo to scientists, so they could study and learn about the animals.

⬇ The giraffes in London Zoo are kept in large, open enclosures rather than being locked up in cages.

Recreating natural habitats

Modern zoos try to balance entertainment for their customers with the welfare of the animals. They create surroundings that are similar to the animals' natural environments. Sometimes these habitats are so realistic that visitors cannot always see the animals!

⬇ Some people argue that animals, such as rhinos, do not belong in zoos in the middle of cities.

Conservation

Many zoos today also try to save endangered species. They do this by breeding them in captivity and then releasing the animals back into the wild.

Despite this good work, some people feel that zoos are still prisons for animals. They argue that it would be better if more money was spent on protecting the animals in the wild.

Performing sea creatures

As well as zoos, there are now many centres and theme parks devoted to sea life. These centres are criticized in the same way as zoos, because they use captive animals. They defend themselves by pointing out the high standard of care that they provide for their animals.

Sea Life Centres

Sea Life Centres in the UK are very popular with children. Visitors can walk past and even under glass tanks that allow them to see marine animals close up. They give visitors lots of information, so children can learn all about the animals.

⬇ A killer whale performing for the crowd at the Sea World marine park, San Diego, USA.

Sea World

The Sea World Adventure Parks in the USA are much larger, and they have some of the biggest marine creatures. There are rides, shows and attractions that star many different creatures, including whales, walruses, seals, polar bears, sea lions and dolphins.

⬇ A young boy watches dolphins swim by in an aquarium tank. Places like this are rather like underwater zoos.

Cruelty or kindness?

Some people think that these parks are cruel, because the animals need much more space than the parks can offer. Sea World argues that its animals are looked after well and enjoy what they do. Sea World also helps with captive breeding.

CASE STUDY ▸ CASE STUDY ▸ CASE STUDY ▸ CASE STUDY ▸

Catherine Mason and her Brownie group visited her local Sea Life Centre in Tynemouth, UK for a sleepover. Catherine said: 'It was great, we slept in the hotel next to the centre and were allowed in to the centre at night. They switched all the lights off except in the tanks — it was beautiful. We learned a lot about fish and they even let us stroke the rays.'

Hunting and fighting

Hurting animals for fun is not as common as it once was. As people have watched and studied animals more, they have come to realize how much pain and distress animals can feel.

Badger-baiting

Badgers are timid creatures, so they are rarely seen. They live in small groups in underground tunnels called setts. Badger-baiting was once a popular activity in the UK. Badgers would be captured and dogs would be set on them, and people would come to watch this show. Badger-baiting was made illegal in 1835, but even today it is still practised in secret.

⬇ These people are watching a cock fight in a market in Thailand. Many bet on the result of the fight.

It is difficult to know why people do this. Many spectators bet on the outcome of the fight, but most just seem to enjoy the bloody spectacle.

⬆ This pitbull dog is forced to walk on a treadmill in order to build up its stamina and strength for fighting.

Dog-fighting

Another cruel pastime is dog-fighting, in which specially bred and trained dogs fight in a ring. It has been made illegal in most Western countries but, like badger-baiting, fights are still carried out secretly in many places.

During a dog-fight, people place bets on which dog will win the fight, but the major enjoyment seems to be from just watching the two animals fight. Usually both dogs are badly injured and, quite often, one is killed in a fight. The RSPCA and ASPCA, which campaign to stamp out dog-fighting, often have to treat the injured dogs, which are abandoned by their owners.

Fox-hunting

Until recently, fox-hunting with horses and dogs was very much a way of life in rural parts of the UK. Many people campaigned to have this practice banned, though. Opponents said that people should not be allowed to gain pleasure from watching an animal being torn to pieces by hounds.

⬇ A huntsman and his fox hounds before the practice was banned.

Fox-hunting supporters

The supporters of fox-hunting argued that their opponents did not understand country ways and traditions. They claimed that foxes were pests that often killed hens, pheasants and even lambs. They believed that hunting was a way of controlling a vicious animal.

They also argued that the hunts created jobs for people, and helped take care of the countryside by maintaining and preserving the areas that were used for the hunts.

The ban on fox-hunting

In 2004, a law was passed in Britain that banned fox-hunting. Many people were angry that they were no longer able to hunt, but others were pleased that this 'sport' had been outlawed.

Fox-hunting is still practised in other countries, including Australia, Canada, France and Italy.

⬆ A fox bares its teeth as the hounds close in for the kill.

⬅ These people are protesting about the ban on hunting. Although many people thought hunting should be allowed, the law against it was passed in 2004.

Trapping animals

Many animals are hunted and trapped for their skin or fur. Hunters use steel traps that snap shut on an animal's leg, breaking or dislocating it. The trapped animal usually suffers agony as it tries to free itself. Some animals have even been known to gnaw through their own legs to break free. Often, animals that are not the target of the hunters are caught in these traps, so their bodies are just thrown away.

The furs, or pelts, recovered are made into coats and other fashion garments. A number of animal-welfare organizations campaign against this kind of fur-trapping. They hope to have the law changed to make it illegal.

⬇ A coyote caught in a leg trap in New Mexico, USA. Hunters trap animals and sell their skins to the fur trade.

The seal harvest

The annual seal-hunt in Canada has caused a huge international outcry. The Canadian government and the hunters say that the seal-hunt is a type of a harvest, rather like fishing, and that it helps keep seal numbers down.

'It takes up to 40 dumb animals to make a fur coat. But only one to wear it.'

SLOGAN ON A GREENPEACE POSTER OPPOSING THE FUR TRADE

Fears for seal survival

There are others who disagree. They are worried that the hunters are killing too many seals and that the population may decline. They are also concerned at the cruelty of the hunt, but the hunters argue that people are just being sentimental about 'cuddly' animals.

 Fur is still part of the fashion scene, but many designers now think that wearing animal skins is cruel and outdated.

Losing natural habitats

Perhaps the most cruel thing humans can do to an animal is make it extinct. Although extinction can happen naturally, humans cause extinction, too. For example, experts believe that early humans hunted mammoths and mastodons to extinction.

 The dodo, a large flightless bird, was hunted to extinction about 350 years ago.

The dodo

Portuguese sailors and the animals that they introduced to the island of Mauritius hunted a flightless bird called the dodo to extinction in the seventeenth century. In North America, the passenger pigeon was hunted to extinction in the nineteenth and early twentieth centuries.

⬇ Cutting down forests for timber can destroy animals' natural habitats.

Destruction of natural habitats

The growing number of people on Earth is the greatest threat to animals. With over half the human race living in cities, we need more space for building.

As we build on open land, mine for minerals, cut down trees for timber and use more land for farming, we take space away from wild animals. These activities destroy the habitats that they need to survive. If they have nowhere to live, these wild animals eventually die out.

⬇ A zoo project has saved the endangered Mauritius kestrel.

CASE STUDY ▸ CASE STUDY ▸ CASE STUDY ▸ CASE STUDY ▸

Modern zoos often work to protect endangered species. Animals at risk are bred in zoos and, where possible, released into the wild, helping to save them from extinction. The Jersey Zoo in the Channel Islands was one of the first to use this approach. In the 1970s, there were only four Mauritius kestrels left in the wild. Now, with the help of the Durrell Wildlife Conservation Trust, there are more than 800 kestrels flying in the skies above Mauritius.

The threat to sealife

Marine animals are among the most threatened by habitat loss. Our ports, cities and factories cause pollution in coastal areas. Large ships and ocean liners dump waste into the sea, which harms creatures in the open ocean.

⬇ The oceans are filled with life, but even marine creatures are affected by human activity and pollution.

Some of the most easily harmed animals are whales. These big creatures are very sensitive to noise and pollution. They will soon leave an area if they are disturbed.

Save the whales

Pacific gray whales were once common, but now they have been hunted nearly to extinction. They migrate between their feeding grounds off Alaska to the lagoons off Mexico's coast, where they give birth.

When a company called ESSA announced plans to open a salt-manufacturing plant at the lagoons where the whales give birth, many people were worried. They were afraid that the noise of pumps and pollution from the plant would drive away the whales. Ships entering and leaving the harbour might hit the whales. There were concerns that loss of habitat might even drive the whales to extinction.

At first, ESSA would not change its plans. The company said that people were exaggerating the threat. But people all over the world began campaigning to protect the lagoons, and ESSA finally agreed to cancel its plans.

⬆ Tourists watch a Pacific gray whale at the Mexican lagoons.

Creating parks for wildlife

One solution to habitat loss is to create national parks. These are places where development is banned so that natural habitats are protected. There are now hundreds of national parks all over the world, which provide a refuge for wildlife.

Risks of national parks

As more and more visitors go to the parks to see 'real' nature, they risk damaging the habitats and the animals that live there. In some US national parks, for example, bears are changing their feeding habits because they have become used to being fed by tourists.

FACT

A recent study by the US Nature Conservancy showed that around 33 per cent of US animal species are at risk of extinction.

⬇ National parks allow people to be close to wildlife, but this is not necessarily a good thing for the animals.

Qomolongma Nature Reserve

One of the largest national parks in the world is the Qomolongma Nature Reserve in Tibet. It is unusual because 75,000 people actually live in the park. The people who run it felt that the best way to protect endangered species was to find ways for humans and animals to live together.

The reserve has been split into zones. Development work is allowed in some of these zones, but not in others. In this way, the future of the fully protected areas is guaranteed. The reserve has been so successful that others are being planned.

⬆ The creation of a huge national park in Tibet has provided a safe home for the endangered snow leopoard.

Ready to act

You may have noticed on the labels of some cosmetics or cleaning products the words 'Not tested on animals' or 'Cruelty free'. These products are now very popular, as more people are taking a stand against animal testing.

Why must products be tested?

The people who make cosmetics and cleaning products have to test these products to make sure they are safe before they can sell them to the public. For a long time, many make-up and household products were tested on animals in laboratories. Some animals, including dogs, cats, rats, rabbits and monkeys, were bred specifically for this purpose.

⬇ Animals, such as rats, are used in laboratories to test the safety of many household products before they are put on sale to the general public.

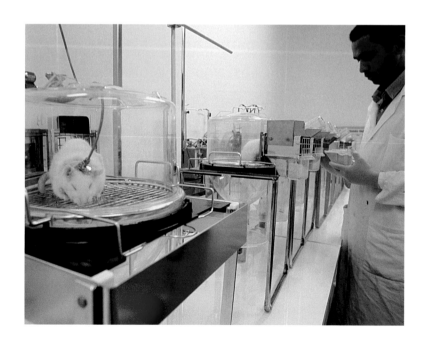

Animal testing

The tests may involve dripping the product on to the animal's eyes or skin. Animals may be force-fed or made to inhale the substance being tested. Many of the tests cause side-effects in the animals. Some can even kill them.

'To my mind the life of the lamb is no less precious than that of a human being. I should be unwilling to take the life of the lamb for the sake of the human body. I hold that the more helpless a creature, the more entitled it is to protection by man from the cruelty of man.'
MOHANDAS K. (THE MAHATMA) GANDHI

Cruelty or not?

Scientists who do animal testing say they are acting for the benefit and safety of us all, but other people believe that the tests are cruel and unnecessary. The testing of cosmetics on animals is now illegal in the European Union.

← These campaigners have dressed up in cow costumes to protest at the treatment of cattle infected by BSE or 'Mad Cow Disease'.

Animal testing for medicine

The most common use of animal testing is for medical products, especially drugs used to treat people who are ill. In most countries now there are laws that make sure the animals used do not suffer unnecessarily. Many drug companies reduce testing to a bare minimum.

Animal rights

People who are against animal testing believe that it should stop altogether. They think it is wrong to inflict cruelty on animals just for human benefit. They also say that there are alternatives to using animals, such as computer modelling and the use of synthetic and cloned human skin for testing products.

⬇ Although animal testing for cosmetics is banned in the European Union, it is still allowed in many countries, including the USA.

Protests

The UK company Huntingdon Life Sciences (HLS) is one of the world's largest companies using animals for testing. It carries out work for many large companies that make products such as medicines, chemicals for farming and food additives.

44

Protestors have tried to close down the company. They draw attention to its activities, and some protesters have even sent threats to HLS employees and attacked their property. The company says that its work saves lives and that it cares for its animals. It is also looking into alternatives to animal testing.

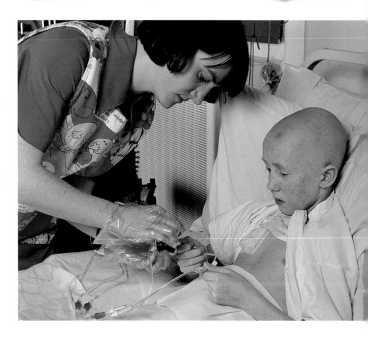

Rights and wrongs

The arguments about animal testing take us back to the questions asked at the beginning of this book. Is it cruel to use animals in this way? That is something that you must think about carefully and answer for yourself.

⬆ Supporters of animal testing point out that it helps companies produce life-saving drugs.

FACT

In 2006, there were more than three million testing procedures carried out on animals in the UK. More than three-quarters of this number were mice (69 per cent) and rats (13 per cent). The next-largest proportion — about nine per cent — were tests made on fish. Mammals other than rats and mice made up four per cent, and reptiles and amphibians around one per cent.

Commission of the European Communities, 2007.

GLOSSARY

Ancient Egypt

The civilization based around the River Nile in what is now Egypt, which lasted from around 3000 BC until around AD 300.

Aquarium

A display of glass tanks containing fish and other marine and freshwater animals and plants.

Baiting

Teasing animals or using cruel methods to make them perform for entertainment.

Campaigner

A person who tries, through argument and direct action, to persuade people to change their attitude to something.

Carnivores

Animals and, very occasionally, plants that eat or absorb meat.

Charities

Organizations that help people or animals in need.

Conservation

Working to protect wildlife and the environment.

Domestic

Trained or raised to be used to live in homes or in the company of people.

Extinction

The death of the last member of a species of animal or plant.

Habitat

The natural surroundings and the conditions in which animals and plants live.

Hatchery

A place where eggs are hatched.

Humane

Caring behaviour that causes the least possible suffering.

Intensive farms

Places or buildings where as many farm animals as possible are kept – the number of animals allowed and the conditions in which they are kept are controlled by law.

Ivory

The material from which tusks are made. Trading in ivory objects is illegal.

Lagoon

A small area of water cut off from the open sea.

Mammals

A class of fur- or hair-covered animals that suckle their young with milk; includes humans, whales, dogs and cats.

Menagerie

A place where captive animals are kept, usually not as big or well-organized as a zoo.

Migrate

To travel long distances, usually in search of warmer weather for feeding or breeding.

Pelt

The skin of an animal with the fur still on it.

Pilot whales

Medium-sized whales that live in groups that follow a leader or 'pilot'.

Refuge

A place of shelter, where animals are protected.

Reptiles

A class of animals that includes snakes and crocodiles.

Vet/veterinary

Vet is a shortened form of veterinarian, a person who performs veterinary work, which means the medical care of animals.

Zoo

A short form of zoological garden, which is the term used to describe a place where animals are kept for display.

FURTHER?INFORMATION

ORGANIZATIONS

These are all reputable organizations that promote strongly held beliefs about animal welfare. Occasionally they show pictures of cruelty to animals, which may be disturbing.

UK

IFAW UK and IFAW Charitable Trust
87–90 Albert Embankment
London SE1 9UD
Tel: 020 7587 6700
http://www.ifaw.org

PDSA
Whitechapel Way
Priorslee, Telford
Shropshire TF2 9PQ
Tel: 01952 290999
http://www.pdsa.org.uk

RSPCA
Enquiries Service
Wilberforce Way
Southwater
Horsham
West Sussex RH13 7WN
Tel: 0300 1234 555
http://www.rspca.org.uk

Worldwide Fund for Nature – UK
Panda House
Weyside Park
Godalming
Surrey GU7 1XR
Tel: 01483 426 444
http://www.panda.org

USA

The American Humane Association
63 Inverness Drive East
Englewood, CO 80112-5117
Tel: 800 227 4645
http://www.americanhumane.org

The American Society for the
Prevention of Cruelty to Animals
424 East 92nd Street
New York, NY 10128
Tel: 212 876 7700
http://www.aspca.org

The Humane Society of
the United States
2100 L Street, NW
Washington, DC 20037
Tel: 202 452 1100
www.hsus.org

The International Fund for Animal
Welfare Headquarters
290 Summer Street
Yarmouth Port, MA 02675
Tel: (508) 744 2000
http://www.ifaw.org

Other useful websites

These websites seek to persuade you that their opinions are right. They use persuasive and, sometimes, emotional language, so read them carefully and make up your own mind on the issues they raise.

Animal Aid
http://www.animalaid.org.uk

Circuses.com
http://www.circuses.com

Compassion in World Farming
http://www.ciwf.co.uk

Dr Hadwen Trust – Humanity
in Research
http://www.drhadwentrust.org.uk

FactoryFarming.com
http://www.farmsanctuary.org/issues/
factoryfarming/

FURTHER READING

In the News: Cruelty to Animals
By Adam Hibbert
(Watts, 2005)

*Protecting Our Planet: Habitats and
Wildlife in Danger*
By Sarah Levete
(Wayland, 2009)

INDEX